with the **WIND**

ADVANCE PRAISE

"Sam Chelanga epitomizes resiliency, compassion and selfless service to all. Sam recognizes that his value is much bigger than how fast he can place one foot in front of the other but rather how his greater impact on others is through his heart and mind. I have been fortunate to be one of many inspired by Sam and his story. His story will cause you to seek and apply your value wherever you are for a greater good."

—Milford H. Beagle, Jr.,
Brigadier General, United States Army

"Sam shows us that running teaches beautiful lessons about life. He shares his journey in vivid detail, making the reader feel like we are in the race with him."

—Emma Coburn,
Olympic Bronze Medalist
and World Champion in the steeplechase

"Sam Chelanga was an amazing runner and is an even more amazing person. His extraordinary humility and depth of soul shine out of his story. Interesting to me, he writes nothing about his many dominant races, like the 2009 NCAA national cross-country championship in which he was ahead of the entire field by forty-two seconds at 8000m. When I asked him why he didn't include any such races, he responded that he didn't learn anything from those races.

Sam's unusual visual clarity and understanding of truth infuse his writing to challenge you, the reader, to run with the wind, whatever your calling in life. Get ready to be inspired to live your life on a higher plane and to run for the stars."

—Brant Tolsma,
thirty-four years as head track coach at Liberty University

"*With the Wind* demonstrates and explains a man's journey to finding joy and freedom. Sam has navigated his way through the pain and pleasure of life and racing, all the while becoming a champion leader along the way."

—Carrie Tollefson,
2004 Olympian, US Champion, TV Analyst

"From the moment I met Sam Chelanga, I could tell he wasn't like other runners. Despite his incredible performances—including one of the greatest careers ever by a collegiate distance runner—Sam has always viewed himself as much more than an athlete. During his incredible life journey, which began when he was plucked from obscurity in Kenya by Paul Tergat, Sam has spent more time than most pondering his purpose and place in the world. *With the Wind* shares the lessons he's learned, from Baringo County to Fort Jackson, S.C., and everywhere in between."

—Jonathan Gault,
staff writer for LetsRun.com

"I enjoyed following Sam's journey through the running world. Seeing behind the scenes of memorable races was really interesting, as he lets us in on his thoughts, values and lessons picked up along the way."

—Molly Huddle,
two-time Olympian and American record holder

"In *With the Wind*, Sam Chelanga offers us a wise and poignant reminder that in seeking to become better athletes, what we truly seek—or should seek—is to become our best selves."

—Matt Fitzgerald,
author of *Running the Dream*

"Sam Chelanga's greatness is not measured by the records he holds, his ascent from poverty, or even by his admirable service in the U.S. Military. Sam's life story is inspiring because it is one of unshakable faith and determination to carry out God's will in his life. *With the Wind* is a handbook on how to live an honorable, fulfilling life, and a reminder that the greatness he displays is found in all of us, if we choose to follow it."

—Jerry Falwell,
President of Liberty University

"Sam's story of transformation and resilience is an inspiration to all Americans. Through words of strength and devotion, Sam brings hope at a vital moment for our nation. He embraces joy on and off the track—a true American hero!"

—Lopez Lomong,
two-time Olympian and Author of *Running for My Life*

"*With the Wind* is an inspirational and exhilarating read. Sam Chelanga exhorts us to reach for the greatness that's already in us all."

—Rashad Jennings,
NFL RB and Author of best seller, *The If in Life*

"Running paved Sam's way from a small village North of Nairobi, but the true essence of his journey was a passage to a bigger world. *With the Wind* is a beautiful and vivid read that all people can relate."

—Bart Yasso,
Retired Runner's World Chief Running Officer

"Running can improve self-esteem and confidence, promote teamwork and goal setting in life... Sam Chelanga's great story of coming from a remote village in rural Kenya to becoming a four-time NCAA Champion, will inspire you. This book has the ingredients to improve anyone's success in life."

—Larry Rawson,
four-time Emmy award Track and Field commentator,
NCAA TV commentator for 51 Championships, and
103 Boston, Chicago, and New York City Marathons

"I loved following Sam Chelanga's running career, and it was a pleasure to get to know more about his background, from the chance encounter in rural Kenya that set him on a course to becoming a professional athlete, to his decision to become a soldier in the United States Army."

—David Epstein,
Author of best sellers, *Range* and *The Sports Gene*

with the
WIND
finding victory within

SAM CHELANGA

NEW YORK

LONDON • NASHVILLE • MELBOURNE • VANCOUVER

With the Wind

Finding Victory Within

© 2020 Sam Chelanga

Published in New York, New York, by Morgan James Publishing. Morgan James is a trademark of Morgan James, LLC. www.MorganJamesPublishing.com

ISBN 9781631951527 paperback
ISBN 9781631951534 eBook
Library of Congress Control Number: 2020938318

Cover Design by:
Megan Dillon
megan@creativeninjadesigns.com

Interior Design by:
Christopher Kirk
www.GFSstudio.com

Morgan James is a proud partner of Habitat for Humanity Peninsula and Greater Williamsburg. Partners in building since 2006.

Get involved today! Visit
MorganJamesPublishing.com/giving-back

CONTENTS

Foreword xiii
Preface xv
Acknowledgments xxi
Introduction xxiii

Chapter I: Nairobi 1
Chapter II: Freedom 9
Chapter III: 27:08. 19
Chapter IV: Surrender 31
Chapter V: The Switch 37
Chapter VI: Through the Mud 49
Chapter VII: Chivale 59

Chapter VIII: Under the Sun. .67
Chapter IX: To See the Heart. 75
Chapter X: Simplicity. 81
Chapter XI: What is Success? 87
Chapter XII: The Call to Serve 95

Afterword. 105
Conclusion 109
About the Author 113

FOREWORD

Sam Chelanga is no ordinary young man. In his journey from the humble beginnings of Saimo Hills in the remote part of Kenya in Baringo County to his lofty placing, donning the jungle Green in the US Army as a Second Lt Platoon Leader at Fort Jackson, SC; Sam has defined determination to another level. He is both inspirational and phenomenal.

I saw something special in Sam from his confident posture and outlook. He looked thirsty for something better, higher. But in between he saw and encountered incredible barriers. Yet Sam did not allow these to dampen his spirit. When I suggested to him of his huge running potential, which was simply out of his least considered options to success, he gave it a go, turning a blind eye to the possible drawback of training with the galaxy of experienced runners and focusing on his goal. That is what makes him different—a go getter.

I am exceedingly proud to have identified, motivated and mentored Sam towards a running and college scholarship, which he has turned into an exemplary tool for personal and community growth. The novel and noble decision to chronicle his outstanding journey so far by authoring this book, *With the Wind* offers an opportunity to inspire contemporaries and generations to have a self-faith, focus and purpose to aspire and reach something bigger for themselves and society.

Without hesitation, Sam's story provides a fresh breath of air and possibilities available to our athletes and young people to become all-rounded in knowledge and service to humanity. *With the Wind* is a story told in fact and thrill, creating in the reader a longing to journey with the star of the story without stopping. Very motivational.

—PAUL TERGAT,
two-time Olympic silver medalist,
five-time IAAF World Cross Country Champion,
President of the Kenyan Olympic Committee,
Kenyan Air Force Officer, and IOC member.

PREFACE

The man sits in solitude, rocking slowly with the movement of waters beneath his small wooden boat. He sees only the lake and the trees that surround him. He went out sailing that day. The winds died down and he sits there now in wait as he looks up to the vast open sky.

Shall he continue to wait, listen and feel for a soft breeze moving in a different direction? Or, will he find the need to paddle in search of the wind that will push him toward where he wants to go? Will he feel the urgency to hunt the wind to fill his sails?

Why does man feel he must move? Was there not beauty in the rocking slowly on the waters beneath the vast open sky? Surely, there must have been. A sail is created to capture the wind and use its strength to propel the boat forward. He must either be still and move with the winds that come, or he must hunt it down. The thing with wind that one must see is that it is only a current of air moving faster than the rest. The air is the same. Why must man seek so hard to fill his sail when the air he really needs was there all along?

I was content in my small village that lay in the Rift Valley of Kenya. I was happy. I had purpose in where I was and with the people in my life. However, after high school, I found myself in unfamiliar territory. A depressed state came over me. It took months to overcome that struggle. Those days of depression went like this: It started with a look. It was ignited by the sight of another. I saw age mates leaving for universities and coming back with degrees. I watched as they strolled those dirt roads in their fancy suits. I heard them chatting over tea about their accomplishments. I observed how they were being treated differently, how others admired them and gravitated toward those who were graduates.

It was as if I was learning that one is no longer enough without that piece of paper. I then believed that if I didn't have it, then I would never be enough. I would become a disappointment and a failure. I had created in my own mind a preconceived notion that I needed to have a college degree and the lack of it would shine a bad light on myself and my family.

Pride. If only I had never told myself that lie and had realized it was my own jealousy that was leading me to my depression. It was me who was reading the script that the world was dictating to me. I was grasping to a false truth that there was something I needed to obtain in order to find worth within myself.

It stems from selfishness. It stems from pride. The reason we depress the higher we go is that we now have to build this idea we have created. To believe something makes one worth more and better, it must be sustained. In essence, one must create his own wind and also keep that current of air flowing. He must continually work at it and force the airs in his direction.

Tom found a quarter. He loved that quarter and used it. When he saw a man by the road, he gave it to him to enjoy. They were both happy. Now a man named Jim, saw the man by the road with the quarter. Jim wanted the quarter and thought he needed it. He hunted one down. He was now not just Jim. He was Jim, with a quarter. Jim saw a man by the river, but didn't want to give him his quarter because Jim believed he needed it. He no longer thought he was enough without it. Jim would do anything to keep his quarter. One day Jim was hiking and found another quarter. Now he had two. Why could he not now give one to the man by the river? Because, Jim must continue to build his idea that his worth lays in the quarters he holds. Therefore, the more quarters he has, the more worth he has. The quarters were what were filling and defining him. He would then do everything he could to preserve and protect them.

How can one look in a mirror and not like the image looking back at them? It is only an image isn't it? To not like the reflection means he is expecting to see something that isn't there. What is he expecting to see? Is he hoping to see something he built? Is he hoping that the image he was trying to create is then shown? Meaning, who he wants to be, should be visible from the outside. He is trying to fit himself into the mirror he created.

Man cannot fit into a world that isn't his. It only leads to feeling stuck. There is a distortion that one air is different than another. We begin to forget that we all came into this world naked. Nothing we add or take away can change that. May we see each other in that way. No lens over our eyes can alter the man that you see. Most of all, may we see ourselves in that way.

I was given a pair of shoes and told to run as fast as I could around a track a bunch of times. I did and I did it faster than everybody. I was then told I was the best. Running faster than everyone else somehow was supposed to make me great. I was then treated better and made to feel I was worth more. If only I could freeze the two images of myself; one from when I was tilling land in the village, and one of me crossing the line and breaking the NCAA 10,000-meter record. I am still Sam. How can a race make me different from within? My worth can surely not be held in a pair of shoes or a time on a race clock. I believe the champion is within us all.

Everyone wants to be happy. Everyone wants joy. I wrote this book to help us to remember where to look for it. What we will see is that we don't have to look very far. I hope these pages will help the reader find the champion in his or her own story.

ACKNOWLEDGMENTS

I would like to thank everyone that I have met on my journey. You mean more to me than you may realize. Thank you to Morgan James Publishing, Jerry Falwell and those who have helped me get these words out to share and hopefully uplift anyone who reads them. My deepest appreciation goes out to my beautiful wife and wonderful boys.

INTRODUCTION

Born in a small remote village in Saimo Hills, Kenya, Sam Chelanga is now a name known by many. Motivated to help his family, Sam literally ran his way out of poverty. With a college running scholarship in America, Sam began his path toward becoming one of the fastest long-distance runners in the world. The highlight of his college career was his 27:08 NCAA Division I 10,000-meter record ran in 2010 that still stands today. He also won four NCAA Division I national titles. As a professional athlete, his accolades include running the second fastest indoor 5k time ever run in United States history with a time of 13:04. He

Chapter I

NAIROBI

I stood in line at the gate of the United States Embassy in Nairobi, Kenya. I fought the glare of the rising sun as I glanced towards the American flag. It was waving high on the pole in the courtyard in front of the building. It was my fourth time at that gate and my chances of receiving that visa were becoming more and more slight by the minute. Each time I stood in line, when it came to my turn, something always went wrong. The wrong paperwork, I was missing something, I needed to have brought a different form or document. This time my problem was time. My classes were to start the next day in the United States and I was still waiting at the gate of the US Embassy in Nairobi. My hopes were low before my turn even arrived.

"Next." The clerk motioned me up to his desk.

Sure enough, there was my moment. As quickly as I was able to muster up some hope, it was shot back down. It was a glimmer of light that quickly dimmed. As I riffled through my folder of documents and forms, he said, "Sir you must have already had travel arrangements made. It is not possible for you to make it to your classes on time. You will have to write to your school in America and tell them you will have to wait until next semester."

I was crushed. I just pictured all of those hours I spent at that small internet cafe in Nairobi staring at the screen hitting the refresh button over and over just waiting in hopes for an appointment slot to open. Even if I tried my luck again, it would be too late. Next semester would not work. My scholarship was based on my ability to run and my first race was just days away.

I didn't know there was another depth to rock bottom. When I started this running thing, I was already at what I felt was my lowest point. My mind immediately turned to the life I would resort back to. I would simply give up on these big dreams I had and be happy to go back to my peasant life. Trying to chase this thing was harder than being satisfied with my humble life. I would be happy to go take care of my dad, the homestead, tend to the cows, till the land, and all that basic subsistence farming entailed.

As I felt myself giving up, all I could think about was a conversation I had with my sister.

"You have potential," she said.

"It doesn't take much to feed me Winnie. I can survive on my own." I replied.

"It's not just about you Sam. If you don't go and dare to dream, who else will? We need someone in our family to make a difference. We need you. You are our hope," she said.

Defeated at the thought that I had failed her and everything that I believed in, I walked outside. It felt like my world had crumbled as I headed out into the unknown. I could feel the sound of the doors close behind me in my chest. I called Paul Tergat to tell him it didn't work out. I couldn't believe I had to tell the man that made it possible for me to be the runner that I was becoming, that it wasn't going to work out. He had done so much to get me to this point.

I remember the day when Paul Tergat convinced me to run. Up until that point, I had thought that maybe I could one day help my family and my community by becoming a lawyer and trying to make a difference in that way. I was working on my brother's farm the day when I first met Paul. I saw this tall man enter the wooden gates and ask for my brother. My brother was a marathon runner at that time and had been training with Paul who was a two-time Olympic silver medalist. Paul saw me and encouraged me to help them out on their long runs. I was fortunate in those days to have been right there watching Paul run and assist him with fluids during his training leading up to the Berlin Marathon in 2003, in which he would win and achieve the world record time of 2:04:55. He went on to win the New York City Marathon in 2005 and he is now a high-ranking officer in the Kenyan Air Force as well as the president of the Kenyan Olympic Committee and a member of the International Olympic Committee.

I had wanted to go to a local university at that time to study law and knew that I would never be able to go on my own, but I thought of Paul. I thought maybe he might be able to help me go to school and become a lawyer or something so that I could try to make a difference. I walked up that rocky road in Ngong Hills toward Paul's home. I made my way to his metal gate that spanned the length of the road. Singila, Paul's guard man, answered my knock. His three dogs came running and barking. Singila led me inside where Paul was sitting on the couch by the window. His wife, Monica, served us chai. As we sat sharing a cup of tea he listened as I asked for his help and I felt like he really saw me. Even still though, just when I thought he was going to agree to assist me with school fees, he said no. He told me he already had so many mouths to feed and had a long list of people who depended on him and needed his assistance for fees and other expenses.

He looked me straight in the eye and told me "It doesn't matter anyway; I know you can run." My hopes of attending a local university in Kenya were right then and there off the table. Paul had his sights on something bigger and on something that seemed too far out of my reach. He told me to join the running group he had organized and to join them for training in the evening. I told him that I was scared and thought that I would fail at it miserably. In fact, my older brother, Joshua, had floated the idea of running to me before, but I sternly shot it down. Paul smiled at me and said, "I have your back. If it doesn't work, I will personally see to it that you find your way to college." His idea seemed as crazy to me as it did to all of the guys waiting by the trail watching me jog up to join them that very day. I had said to Paul, "I can't run," and I saw the same sentiment on the faces of those guys I was about to try to keep up with. No one could believe I was going to try to join them for training. I didn't believe it either. I didn't know what I was doing there, except that I was desperate.

All of that led me here. I was at the US Embassy thinking I had made it. I stood at those gates, still helpless. Despite everything we had done and how far we had come. I was so close, yet so far. Doubt was beginning to take root again. I started to think to myself that maybe it wasn't meant to be. I was gut wrenched.

Paul answered the phone. I told him I hadn't gotten the visa. All he said was, "Wait for me right there," and he hung up. I tried walking back to the gate but the security officer kicked me out. I pleaded for him to let me wait. He told me to stand back 100 feet and if someone came looking for me, he would wave me over. Not too long after that, I saw the man in the green army suit with one arm on the rifle by his side waving to me with his other arm. He told me that someone inside had received a phone call on my behalf and that I should go back inside. Again, Paul had my back. I felt the encouragement I needed. Hope was still on the horizon. Paul organized my travel arrangements with my brother and got me on a flight for that very night.

That afternoon felt like a tornado of getting ready for my trip to America. We rushed back to pack my stuff. My cousin gave me a navy-blue Nike duffle bag and I shoved all of the belongings I had in it. My brother gave me a couple pairs of shoes and brought me to get some small supplies that I needed, like toothpaste and what not at the local Nakumart grocery store. He also gave me $500 for pocket money. With that little plastic bag in hand, I, for the first time, knew this was it. I boarded a KLM Airlines plane that night. I took my seat and knew something great was going to happen in my future. I was finally on that plane that I watched fly over the village when I was young. My day dreaming as a little boy had come to fruition. It was now my reality.

Chapter II

FREEDOM

I got off that plane ride at about two o'clock in the afternoon. Three of my new teammates picked me up from the John F. Kennedy airport in New York City and made the drive to Fairleigh Dickinson University in Teaneck, New Jersey. Edwin was one of the guys who came to pick me up. He was from Kenya and understood what I was going through. I cannot thank him enough for orienting me to my new life at FDU. There were so many new sights to take in but I wasn't able to soak in any of them yet. New York City was so big and I didn't recognize anything. It was sensory overload with everything being very different. Then I saw the George Washington Bridge. I had seen that bridge before in a magazine that my brother had brought back from his travels. As we drove over that bridge it hit me. I thought to myself, "It's going down, this is it, I've made it."

I had to be in class in less than four hours. I left my bags in Edwin's car and my new teammates dropped me off at the door just in time for my 6pm class. I remember finding a seat in the back of the room. I didn't hear too much of what the professor was saying. I had to ask him to talk slower sometimes for my English was still a bit rusty. All I could think of though was how relieved I was that I had made it. I had flown from Kenya to America and was sitting in a college class. When I think of it now, it's still quite amazing. I don't know how a little village kid like me was able to come so far. My purpose really was beyond me.

The next two days were a whirlwind of in-processing, getting books, schedules, and learning the campus. Before I knew it, it was the weekend and the cross-country team and I were on a bus to Van Cortland Park in NYC. We pulled into a parking lot that faced a field of green grass and trees that were so colorful. I had never seen foliage like this. I could see the race trail across the way through the myriad of tents set up by all of the different schools. This would be my very first race in the US. Now that I think of it, this would be my very first official race ever. It was eight kilometers long. I had no idea what was in store. What I did know was Paul's sentiments about it. He had prepared me for that very moment. He told me this race was like my interview. I had to deliver. I felt the pressure. My coach told me to start strong and finish strong. I laced up my spikes and followed my teammates to the start line. You could hear all of the feet hitting the gravel trail like the clicking of horseshoes on a racetrack. I could feel the intensity.

The gun went off and so did we. After I sprinted for what I felt was about a minute or two, I couldn't hear anything. I felt like all I could hear was my own breathing. I looked back and there was no one. I had made a significant gap. I kept going and going. I began to doubt it was happening. I thought, "Had I taken a wrong turn?" I was still getting my bearings with sense of direction those days. I started to wonder whether I had mixed up taking the big loop for the small loop. Doubt had won me over and I turned around and started running in the opposite direction to see if I could find the other guys. It wasn't long before I saw a group of the yellow Quinippiac singlets hoofing down the trail toward me. I quickly changed my direction back to the path that I came from and picked up the pace. I finished the big loop, and then the small. I was first to come across the line and had a great finishing time on the race clock. I looked to my coaches and their excitement was evident. I felt a sigh of relief. The pain had been worth it. My efforts had been rewarded.

My days at Fairleigh Dickinson were great. I made friends, was on track for classes and studies, and was making headway in the running world. One race that really put me on the map was the Iona Meet of Champions. It was picked up by the news and I remember my roommate telling me that word was getting around about this fast freshman kid from FDU. I went on to win conference, regionals and finished sixteenth at the National Collegiate Athletics Association Division I national championships in Terra Haute, Indiana. I was breaking school records and had made quite the reputation. People began to know my name. That should've been all I needed. Never would I have thought I could have fallen on such success. I did it. I was on the road to a great college degree in the US, I was winning races and earning medals, I had friends and was having fun. What else could I need at that time? Something in me though was telling me otherwise.

Despite everything going right at Fairleigh Dickinson, I felt as though something was still missing. I was where I was supposed to be. All that we had worked so hard for had come to fruition, and there was no reason to think otherwise. I had an itch though. There was peace, but also a tug that I can't really explain. It was something deep inside me. To try to understand it completely seemed pointless.

It took me back to those days I spent after high school, chasing after the status that I thought would come with a degree. I had remembered those feelings of embarrassment when I had nothing to define me next to my name. I had felt like a nobody, without purpose and significance when I was desiring to be a college graduate simply because I had let pride root itself into my ambitions. The darkness that I had felt in the struggle of feeling lost was far worse than any adversity I had ever experienced in my life. I had thought that losing my mom at such a young age and watching her sickness progress for so long would be the highest point of pain I could ever feel. It was far darker, though, when I felt lost. I think that time in my life woke me up in a way. It taught me to never underestimate that type of struggle. It also taught me to cling to that which satisfies the soul and that which allows one to see clearly.

The journey doesn't have to be easy; it just has to be right. Sometimes as people we need to just be. Content. Free to go where the soul leads. One cannot fit heaven inside their head. We can't try so hard to comprehend. Just as we breathe, we don't think about it, we just do it. The birds don't have food for the day by worrying about it either. We cannot always trust our own understanding for it is limited. We can rather acknowledge that we are in the hands of a higher purpose above our self.

I had reached success in my worldly eyes. Though I was on track with everything I could tangibly touch, I wasn't fulfilled. It was deeper than sense. It was of the soul. This is where one must pay attention. This is why attempting to track down happiness cannot work. This is why striving on one's own self to the nth degree will never fulfill. There has to be a reason for the striving, searching and chasing that is right. I found what I thought I wanted, but there was still a vacancy for happiness. Happiness did not lie where I thought it had.

I kept on going, though, and pushed that vacancy to the back of my mind as I focused on the tasks ahead of me. One of which included getting the qualification for the NCAA Division I Indoor Nationals. I did not know how pivotal that race would be for me. Josh McDougal was a big name in NCAA Cross Country those days. Before the race began, I approached Josh to talk pre-race tactics and pacing thoughts, etc. He told me very confidently that he had it. He was sure he would qualify and didn't need much help. He told me to just sit behind him and push him along. So, I did just that. The race went just as simply as he described it, I crossed the line with a qualifying time and the school's indoor record of 13:46 for the indoor 5,000 meters (3.1 miles). Josh was so kind and such a good man. I thought to myself that there was something different about him. I had to reach out to him. I had the desire to get to know him a bit more. I found him on Facebook and we began chatting now and then.

One day he asked me how I was doing. I admitted to him that I felt stuck and like I was heading nowhere, which I understood didn't make much sense. I was heading somewhere. I had great promise ahead of me, how could I be stuck? I had everything I needed, yet I felt far from satisfied. It was proof that happiness is not dependent on circumstances. McDougal heard me. He understood what I felt. He said, "Well it sounds like you're describing my school." McDougal brought me to Liberty University. That is where my journey really began to break headwind. I stepped out and I chose to dismiss all those who told me not to transfer schools. I decided to ignore any hindrance in my way and move to Lynchburg, Virginia. For I knew my call, what made sense for my soul. Though it was what could be seen as failure to one, it was right for me. Something deeper than the surface had to be filled.

We must not fear failure. For the success one must strive for cannot be judged by another man. Therefore, neither can failure. You only need one cow to lead the rest. I had a cow named Cheptuya. No matter where or what the circumstances were, if I could direct my lead cow Cheptuya, the rest would follow. Our road cannot be determined by the rest. Success and failure are subjective. Subjective to everything. To everyone. Each one of us has our own road, our own journey. Therefore, to compare is more senseless than just following a cow. Simply, one shoe doesn't fit all.

Chapter III

27:08

I t was spring of 2010, at Liberty University. I was training for the Payton Jordan 10,000-meter race at Stanford University, which was just a few weeks away. Preparations had been going well and I had logged some serious miles on those beautiful Virginia mountains. My fitness was right where it needed to be. Many use the race to get some fast times in so I knew I needed to be sharp. I had been working on my speed at the track. I was averaging about 2:45 for 1 km repeats, 2:10 to 2:05 for 800s, and 4:20 to 4:35 for mile repeats.

On one Sunday morning, after a week of working hard on repeats at the track, I went out for a long run. I drove about thirty minutes outside of Lynchburg to run on this beautiful road called Rocky Mountain Road. It's truly just you, the trees and the deer out there. Perfect for my 14-18 miler. Not many people know about this spot for running. It is a hidden gem. You just find a discreet spot to park your car along the edge of the windy road. I like to park near this creek that runs down from the mountain. I was feeling good so I remember pushing hard somewhere around about 6:30 to 5:30 minutes per mile pace. I was moving through those hills and windy turns feeling like a gazelle.

I'm often asked whether I like to listen to music when I run or what I think about for so long while running. Eighteen miles would be about one hour and forty minutes to two hours or so out there on the trails. I can strongly tell you though, that I do not like listening to music when I run. Nor do I spend my time in much thought at all. It is more like a rest out there on the trails and the road. I find running very therapeutic. I feel the rhythm of my feet working and the motion of my arms pushing through the landscape. Every mile I drive, but only with my legs. My mind is completely at rest. As I was working on that symphony in the woods, and pushing that pace, I took a turn somewhere around the eleventh mile and my stride landed my foot right on a rock. As my metatarsals hit the peak of the stone and went to go forward for the next stride, I felt something move. Something tweaked in my foot, but with a few more strides it adjusted and I was able to finish the run with no problem.

I forgot all about my foot hitting that rock until the next morning when I took my first step out of bed onto the floor of my apartment. I felt a soreness shoot right through the top of my foot. Something definitely felt wrong. I thought I should have it checked out by our school physical therapist. Sure enough, it turned out I got a stress reaction in my left foot.

I told my coach the diagnosis and without hesitation he said I had to take a break. I was bummed, but knew there was really no other option. Time was running out and I had to qualify for nationals. I needed to be ready by Payton Jordan on May 3rd, 2010. There was nothing I could do though, pushing through the injury would only bring me to the race line injured even further. It was going to be tight. It was less than a month before the race and I would need to dial it back significantly.

I did as coach told me and lightened up my training a lot. I was basically just sustaining. I didn't push speed and cut my mileage to only twenty to thirty miles a week. I was beginning to miss out on key workouts. Coach told me that Alberto Salazar, the head coach for the Nike Oregon Project, had called asking if I could help Galen Rupp. He was one of his star athletes and was looking to break the American record. They needed a pacer near the end to push Galen to the finish. I told coach that it was an exciting opportunity, however my confidence was very low with my injury. I really wanted to help, but I was unsure that my foot would hold. My fitness was there, but my training was not. I thought it would be amazing just getting myself to the line able to run and finish the race, never mind trying to help Galen break any type of record.

I tried to keep up with the schedule and do what I could to stay as fit as possible. I prayed for improvement. Sure enough, that is what I got. The last week leading up to the race, I started to feel some slight healing. I was able to get in some sprints and up my mileage just a little.

I was able to gain just enough confidence that I would at least be able to put in a good effort come the night of the race. Coach Tolsma, the team and I flew out of Raleigh, North Carolina to San Francisco for the Stanford Invite at Palo Alto, California. Track races often have multiple heats, meaning the race is divided into groups. Heat one was usually the fastest group of runners and heat three, for example, would usually go a bit slower. I had originally planned on going in the faster heat for the race. However, with my foot being compromised and my training having not been what it should've been, coach Tolsma thought it would be smarter to take it easy and run in the second heat. Even though my foot was feeling slightly better it did not seem wise to push it and risk ruining my entire season by running too hard too soon, let alone going on American record pace. We landed in San Francisco past midnight and went straight to the hotel to get some sleep. When race day had arrived in the morning, nothing felt special. I remember sitting having a club sandwich for lunch feeling quite relaxed.

The vibe at the race hotel was quite hyped though. Galen was aiming to break the American record in the 10k, which was a really big deal. I was out of the conversation. Typically, I would plan to go, give everything, and see what I could get. Physically with my foot, I was not sure what I could do. Without the pressure of having to go for the win or try to make a certain time, I was able to just be thankful that I saw some improvement and was going to be able to race at all. Coach agreed and thought that there was really nothing we could do at that point.

He and I talked casually as we ate our lunch. I began to feel that there wasn't much harm in just taking a risk. I could just give it a go in the first heat. Surely there would be some guys running in the back that I could stick with. I could run behind the lead pack and at least give myself a better chance to finish with a decent time. We weren't 100% sure, but it seemed the better option and just like that, we decided to go for it.

The sun was beginning to go down and that meant that the start time was nearing. During the warm-up, I felt better than I had in the last three weeks. I decided not to do any strides, so as to not flare up anything just before the gun went off. I wanted to save everything for those twenty-five laps around the track that were ahead of me. I started out on my usual twenty-minute warm-up.

About five minutes into it I realized I didn't feel any pain. I couldn't believe it, something had tweaked again, this time in my favor. Something felt different. I didn't feel the soreness I had been feeling. By the time I toed the line that night, I couldn't help but just thank God.

We lined up like horses behind the starting gate ready to storm out. The race official approached and raised his starting pistol aiming it toward the sky. With the loud bang we took off. The pacers sprinted straight to the front and assumed their duty. Just as they had planned, the pace was hot. The leaders were going sixty-four to sixty-five seconds per lap. I hung as tight as I could. After about a mile into it I couldn't believe it, the signs of pain in my foot were nowhere in sight. I took it lap by lap. When I realized my foot was holding up, I said, "I'm ready to move." I could hear the splits for the first time. I couldn't believe I heard someone shout, "That was sixty-four, stay right there." It felt easy for me. It felt like sixty-seven seconds. We were about two miles into the race and my confidence was kicking in.

I said to myself, "Just stay in contact." The pacer hit the splits just right. They were going hard and there were only four or five guys left toward the front. I saw

Chris Solinsky, Simon Bairu, the pacer, Daniel Salel and Galen. They were really going after it. It was one mile to go, then three laps to go. Solinsky was behind me with one other guy and I could feel him on fire. It wasn't long before he passed me and took off into the lead. Bairu was falling back. I was just trying to hang on. My wheels were falling off. I followed as tight as I could. With two laps to go we were all kicking and the gaps were beginning to form. Solinsky had taken a big lead and I could feel myself gaining on Rupp.

As soon as I heard the bell ring on that last lap. I chased them down as hard as I could. I passed Galen and pushed toward the homestretch, having no idea what the time on the clock was. As my feet crossed that line I gazed up to the screen and saw 27:0-something. I couldn't believe my eyes. I couldn't believe how God had blessed me. That was not my performance. I would've been amazed if I were to run any time sub twenty-eight minutes that day. A personal best was way out of my mind. I have no words to fully describe what happened that night. I ran not only a personal best, but with that 27:08, I broke the NCAA Division I 10,000-meter record that still stands today. It was beyond logic.

Being stuck in a box, one will never fully understand its purpose. It isn't until he views it from the outside, that he then can see it in clear view. That race meant more than a record to me. If I was fit and ready to run, if I had that confidence in myself, if I knew I had done everything necessary to run 27:08, when I did it, I don't think I would have felt the same way. It was when I crossed the line that it felt special. Special in that I hadn't done what it took. I wasn't ready. Yet, I walked away having just run what would be the fastest 10k time of my whole college and professional career. It was a different type of happy.

I am literally staring at tubs of shoes right now that lay in the corner of our living room. There are at least twelve tubs that I can see from this angle. Keeping in mind that I have given away countless amounts of running gear and shoes to anyone that has asked and anyone that I thought could use it, these tubs still lay here. After our most recent move to an apartment, while in transition to our next Army duty station, there literally wasn't enough space for it all. Our storage shed and closets are full with all of this top of the line Nike gear that I have received over the years. What I find interesting though, is none of them are too valuable to me. There are some shoes that I wore when I won an epic race. There are a couple that were custom designed, some innovation prototypes, and some that I thought my kids would like to wear in the future. None are so meaningful though, that I cherish them per say. There is a pair however that I did cherish, and that I no longer have.

I was about eight years old when my mom would wake me early in the morning. We would gather our harvest of fruit and vegetables, the supplies she needed to make tea, and about ten to fifteen of those mugs made out of tin and enamel which she would use to serve the tea in. We would hike for miles through the valley. We would trek around dangerous cliffs and through thick woods and would reach the remote market as the sun started to rise. My mom would lay out a mat underneath this big tree and set up shop in hopes that we would sell enough so we could buy supplies and pay school fees. I couldn't help but notice that every week a man would come to sell sandals made out of old tire scraps. I didn't have any shoes at that time and those sandals really caught my eye. I couldn't get them out of my mind. I finally had the guts to ask my mom. I told her, "Please mama, I really want them." I could tell she was thinking about it. "Well, how about you sell the passion fruit next week at the farmers market and if you get enough, you can buy them yourself," she said. I couldn't believe it. So, the next week we woke early and I gathered the fruit as I usually did. We made the trek into the woods, down the windy road to our local farmers market in a small shopping center called Kipsaraman. As the sun rose my heart couldn't help but smile.

When we arrived, we set up our spot. We had a few customers here and there, but the passionfruit were still plenty and my sack of shillings not yet enough. Some local nuns that worked at the Catholic Church in the village nearby were doing their usual shopping. They saw me and came right toward our mat. They asked me what I was up to. My sister claims that I was very smart and quite chatty when I was a little boy. Not sure if that is what happened, but somehow, I explained to them my endeavor and those tire sandals I wanted so eagerly. Well, those nice ladies looked at my pile of passion fruit, and bought them all.

We arrived at our hut late that evening as we usually did, but this time as we entered under our roof, I got to take those sandals off my feet. I put them neatly by the door and knew that was one of the most special gifts I had ever received. I could not have gotten those sandals on my own. It was the meaning in them. They truly did make me happy. Sandals, made out of recycled tires, trump all of the shoes I have worn as an elite over the years.

Chapter IV

SURRENDER

The days I was free to run. I can see those woods so clearly now. The entrance to the path lays hidden alongside of Liberty Mountain Road. One probably wouldn't even see it if they drove by. It was a simple trail not more than two feet wide, but it goes on for miles. Soft Virginia leaves coat the footing. The trees were quiet in those woods. My legs felt like they were dancing around the bends and through those rolling hills. I could feel the mountain and it urging me up. The drive I felt to push because it hurt so good. I could hear my breathing. I could sense the echo of my footsteps. I was free. There is something in doing something purely. I was working harder than I had ever worked. Running more miles than I had ever run. Running for the right reasons and in the right way though, brought a peace out of it.

Before a big race a few of the runners are usually asked to appear the day or evening before for a press conference. They are asked questions about how their training is going and how they think the race will play out the following day. My wife asked me one day why I told everyone my game plan during my interview. She asked me if I wouldn't rather keep my tactics a secret until the race was over. I told her there are no secrets. Even in college I would say exactly what I was going to do. I would tell them, "I am going to take it out very hard and see how it goes." There is a confidence in laying it all out. Free to accept any outcome. Free to just be.

I sat in stillness reclined on the hotel rolling desk chair facing the white wall. My bowl of oatmeal lay beside me in my peripheral vision but my thoughts were elsewhere. I was trying to prepare mentally for the race before me. I had come so far. I was about to finish off my entire time of running in college and NCAA with the one race that was just hours ahead of me. It was my last chance. I had not won the 10k the night before so all that remained was twelve laps around the track.

When race time came and we unloaded the bus at the track. We dropped our gear and went out to warm up. For warm-ups, I usually go about ten minutes out and ten minutes back. This time though, when I got back with the guys and they started stretching, I didn't feel ready. An energy started swirling around me. I said to myself, "I have to go again." I needed to go back and warm up again. So, I took off and went for five more minutes out and back, all the while praying.

My mind and heart were in a wrestle. I felt myself thinking, "This is too much for me." I felt nervous. I felt the pressure. I know I had accomplished so much already, why did I feel these nerves now? I couldn't understand. All I could hear, almost audibly was the saying, "You are only as good as your last race." I realized the pressure of signing an elite contract, impressing agents and companies was already beginning to seep in before my time as a professional had even commenced.

I went out for that warm-up for the second time in a daze. Like in a fog, I could see only my feet striding beneath me. The sea of the runners around me, the tents, the grass, the spectators, were like the blurry background in a movie scene. Then the fog cleared. I heard words being whispered to my soul. "Chill out Sam," "You've done your best," "You're being too hard on yourself," "You don't need to prove anything," "I'm already proud of you." The peace returned and I walked to the track, this time ready for the gun to go off.

Coach Tolsma prayed for me before I went to take my spot on the line. I always start from the front and take off like a bullet, but this race I took a backseat. I said to myself, "Let it go." I wanted to surrender in a way. I felt the need to continue to run in freedom and allow myself not to chase. So, I forced myself to sit back and see how the race would unfold. The runners took off with the gun and I positioned myself in second to last place. As the race progressed, I fought to move into lane one, but no gaps were opening. Like moving a stick shifter into gear, I tried again and again to move in, but there was no gap until I had moved all the way up to first gear and found an opening in fourth place.

I felt the momentum building and I just kept moving and working until it was just me and Lawi Lalang the leader. Lawi was a ferocious freshman who was full of energy and out to destroy the field. I admired and understood his front running style, as that was how I usually preferred to race. I could see him looking for help for he had paced much of the laps. I decided that although I felt tired, I would help. There I found myself where I usually did, in the front. As I felt everyone behind me, I realized, why not give it all? So, I started pushing. The gap began to grow bigger and bigger. When there wasn't anybody beside me anymore and the big screen high above the track projected only me running toward the finish line, I knew I had it. I crossed the line winning my fourth national title and finishing my very last NCAA race.

All I had to do was let go. Even though I had accomplished so much until that point, I almost let the overwhelming thought that everything boiled down to my last NCAA race overtake me. In my mind, I was rationalizing that it was that race that would determine where my future would take me, but that race proved otherwise. We must always remember that we are toeing a line that we've already won. We must approach every challenge with gratitude, appreciating the gift of life and what flows from it. In my experience, the biggest critic was myself.

I beat myself down too hard when I should have been focusing on what was good. We are so often focused on what's next and wanting more that we forget to meditate on the good that already is. As I was busy scheming for the next chapter in my running, I was reminded that the future is not mine to scheme. It was in the letting go that propelled me to that finish line feeling completely fulfilled. The truth is, we must slow down and enjoy the moments we're in, big or small, for tomorrow will take care of itself. Happiness flows from inside out. We must therefore cultivate it from the inside and allow it to blossom from outside.

There is a war to fight. There is a battle of spirit. We must stand guard and hold true. The battle to succumb to despondency, inadequacy, and disbelief is right where defeat wants us. We must not lay feeble, but must instead summon the light inside us. We must stand in acknowledgement and in fight. This is the truth. Our happiness will be marred and hidden by darkness unless we rip away from it. We are always free to run free, despite what the scenery may look like.

Chapter V

THE SWITCH

My college days seemed to be quickly fading behind me as I was thrust into the world of elite running. The summer nights were filled with fun and the horizon looked awfully bright. The phone calls and email correspondence with my agent were nonstop though. As we were deciding on and negotiating contracts, I was slowly beginning to realize that running free may become more and more of a difficult thing to hold on to.

One of my first races as a professional was the Beach to Beacon 10k in Cape Elizabeth, Maine. The race takes place in what I would consider one of the most beautiful places in America. Maybe I'm biased because my wife grew up in Cape Cod and we have spent a great deal of time on those northeastern coasts, but I found Cape Elizabeth hard to match. My wife came with me and as we were trying to make the best of this new territory of elite running and enjoy all of its amenities, the pressures were really getting to me and stealing the joy from right beneath my feet.

The seasoned and talented elites, many with impressive resumes, took to the line. The humidity set on my body like a ton of bricks. When we took off at the start, my legs felt like they were twice the size they were and my feet were dragging with every step. I couldn't find my bounce. I couldn't summon the spark. I watched as the leaders slid into the tree lined turn ahead of me. I tried to urge my body to catch up, but I could do nothing except watch them run out of my sight. This race was a foreshadow of what was to come in my years as an elite. It was a constant fight the entire time. I worked the many miles I ran and the many races I won and didn't win. The rewards I got felt only justified for the efforts I put out. Something had changed once I tied all of those strings onto the running that was once free.

As an elite runner, the pressures felt real. I was thrown full throttle into them. I had a difficult time separating the life as an elite and the love of running I knew that was within me. The contract, expectations, schedules, money and all that I was supposed to live up to was overshadowing all I thought the life of an elite would be.

There were glimmers of hope. Like shooting stars when I needed them the most. That kept me going all of those years. They were reminders to stay strong for there was something there worth digging for. I knew I had what it took, I was just riding a one gear bicycle trying to keep up with the three speed I once was.

In 2013, I incurred an injury from pounding the track in Oregon. It was a stress fracture in my right metatarsal and I was sentenced to wearing a boot for six weeks. I couldn't believe it. All of the training, build up, hard miles and repeats now had nothing to show except that oh so fashionable giant boot that I wore like a shackle being dragged around. The worst part of it all, I wasn't that motivated to cross-train and do everything I could to get it off. I realized I had lost so much of my joy in running during those first years as an elite that I couldn't even find the motivation and hurry to get the boot off. I not only felt frustrated, but I knew I needed a change of heart.

I used the opportunity of down time and rest to make a change in my training and location and to try out running the miles with Ben True in Hanover, New Hampshire. He was a good buddy that I had met running races as a pro while I was with Oregon Track Club Elite. There was something about the country boy in him that I thought would help me tap back into the free running I knew was just around the corner for me. My wife and I made that epic cross-country road trip from coast to coast with our little boy Micah, only five months old in the back of our SUV.

It was a new year, a new place, and a new training program. Fresh out of the recovery boot from the injury, I met with Ben and coach Mark Coogan of Dartmouth College. There was something about it. When you think long distance running, you think Arizona, Oregon, Colorado, maybe New Mexico, but rarely does someone think of New Hampshire as a running hub. There is just something about those brisk northeastern woods, though. Ben and I worked those miles up in New England. I remember it like it was yesterday pulling double runs through West Lebanon, New Hampshire. With temperatures only in the teens, we would go for our second run adding miles in the snow. It's a different atmosphere up there. I felt like I belonged.

It's unconventional, but quenching. We would run around three small towns in one run. From West Lebanon, through the woodsy hills, around the ponds and creeks, on the side of the little town center square toward the suburbs of Lyme, down the main road and over the bridge crossing over the Connecticut river into Vermont. Through the streets of the quaint town of Norwich, we slowed down to smell the fresh foods from the local Saturday farmer's market and continued down to the back roads into Hanover. I would clock about eighteen miles. Ben brought back the country boy in me. Those New Hampshire woods and I were one. I vividly remember one of the points over Vermont where Ben and I would stop at the top of this hill and enjoy the commanding views surrounding us. I knew those trails and roads like the back of my hand. I had grown in love with the frigid, iced-over winter, that only led to the melting of spring and the warm, full of life summer.

After training for a bit up there, I had the Dartmouth cross-country meet lined up as my first race after my injury. I was basically just testing how I was holding up. I was quite rusty. However, it was a success in assuring that I was on the right track in returning back to my fitness. After going back to the trails and roads for more mileage, coach Coogan had Ben and I hit the track. We hit it hard. We would run workouts mixing the track with tempo runs on the roads. Coach liked to have us do a specific workout. We would do one mile at around 4:20 per mile pace on the track and then do one mile on the sidewalk around the track at a 6:00 per mile pace. We would repeat the same repetitions of 1200 meters, 800 meters, 600 meters and finally an all-out 400 meters. Sometimes he would change the last rep to one mile at 4:20 per mile pace. I remember the day when we hit the last mile in a 4:15. We skipped the mile jog after the last repetition and headed straight for a three-mile cool down around Occom pond. My favorite workout was doing a three-mile warm-up and cool-down, eight x 400 meters on the track, four-mile tempo at 4:50 per mile pace on the road and back to the track for another eight x 400 meters at sixty-five seconds each with a minute rest in between.

After what felt like a solid training block, coach told me to do an indoor mile race at the Dartmouth invite.

He stressed the need to get my turnover going. It wasn't pretty, but I hit the track and raced with college guys to finish with a time of 4:03. The race was about three days before the 5k Indoor in Boston.

I went into that 5k race not knowing what to expect. Coach Coogan's strategy for me was always speed so I knew I had some turnover in my legs, but that was all I knew. I had no other way to judge my fitness. I was in a completely different training environment and schedule. The workouts were different and my training was just all around new to me. I wasn't sure what I was going to be able to deliver that day. I got to the race and it was like déjà vu: Galen Rupp was going for the American record, this time for the indoor 5k.

Everything was organized. They had pacers. All I had to do was show up and run. I was aiming to run with Cam Levins. He would be behind Galen and I could just shoot for a good time. I gave myself some wiggle room. I thought if I could hit 13:20 as a finishing time that would be a good day. I would walk away happy, knowing that I had been away from the indoor track for a while and it was my first real race of the season. In the back of my mind I knew I had worked really hard that fall and made the best of those many miles on those chilly hills of New Hampshire. It was behind the scenes training and I couldn't judge it or compare it to anything for it was all new to me, but I did know I had been working and working hard.

This was one of the first races I had my son watching. I remember feeling a sense of comfort and ease knowing that my family was there watching and having a good time. Jack Davies had joined Ben and I up in New Hampshire to train with us a month or two before the race. He was always willing to grind it out on the trails with us. He was a guy with outstanding passion and dedication. He was also an excellent teammate. As we stepped outside to do our warm-up, I told him I wasn't sure I was ready but at least I didn't have those bad pre-race nerves. Jack told me he believed in me. He said, "You've been working and MB (my wife) is here. I'm going to be out there. You are probably going to pass me two times, but I'll be cheering for you." He probably doesn't know how much comfort his words gave me. He was a good teammate. I felt good.

We warmed up, I took a sip of my sports drink and got ready to toe the line. I remember walking up next to the competitors feeling as though we were just friends, all approaching the same battle. I was quickly reminded otherwise. We were not on the same side of that battle zone. I looked to one of the competitors and saw in his eyes that this was not going to be a friendly fight, it was going to be war. My mood immediately changed, like the flick of a switch. I felt like the gladiator during the underdog scene. We were in the arena. That was it. I was no longer running with Cam Levins. I was going to race.

I had arrived at the arena aiming to just have fun. I was unsure and not confident in my training and quite timid about my capability that night. In an instant though, I was able to summon the fierce within me. I said, "It's on." I realized I had to stop doubting and putting limits on myself. I was going to stick to Galen as best I could. The gun went off and I tucked right behind Cam and Galen. Two pacers led the three of us split by split. We hit the 2k in 5:17. They were pushing and moving fast. Every time I felt my pace start to slow, I would fight back and maintain contact again. One of the pacers couldn't hold the heat and fell off. Another lap down, and the last rabbit stepped off the track. The race was on. I was feeling it. My legs wanted to move.

My strides were itching to go. Two miles done with only one to go and the clock read 8:26. I could hear the stadium roaring. The pace began to feel too hot to handle. I wasn't sure I could hold it. My mind wanted it more than my legs. Galen started to kick. He moved past the homestretch looking back and he found me following. We hit the laps and I just followed him stride for stride right at his heels. We were flying. I felt like my feet were barely hitting the surface of the track. As I took a moment to breathe, Galen took off. The stadium was roaring. The hype was incredible. I knew we were running fast but I didn't see the clock. I just watched Galen ahead of me and chased him down as fast as I could. He had made a gap but I was still moving. I saw Galen cross the line and I followed just four seconds behind. I had no idea what time I ran. I gave Galen that pat on the back and met my coach in the center of the track.

"Do you know what you just ran?" he said, "13:04!" I couldn't believe it. I just jumped on him. I was so full of joy. All I had to do was believe. I just had to give myself a shot. The same race I had approached with doubt and loss of confidence, led to a race that today is still my personal best and stands as the second fastest American indoor 5k of all time. After cool-down, post-race interviews, and talking to my friends, I exited through the doors of that building much different than when I entered them. The dark evening brings beauty to those Boston streets. My wife, little Micah and I made our way to the hotel led by the light shining down from those Boston lampposts and we were in awe of what had just happened. That was one of the best races of my career.

Looking back now I have to thank Galen for a lot of memories of great racing. We walked away having broken the indoor 5k record. I could've given in to my doubts. I could've held on to the thoughts that were holding me back. "Was I fit enough?" "Could I handle it?" "Was I still in Galen's league?" We need to tap into our potential. We need to realize there is a spirit that surpasses anything we can see. We must walk to every line in life and recognize doubt shall be nonexistent. Ignore any thoughts about limits but allow yourself the freedom to be free.

There is gold in just living. Living, knowing there is confidence within you. We must deny what tries to keep us down and realize we are already enough. We must see it is not about the race at all. It is about how one sees it and how one sees themselves in it. What you seek, you will see. May we seek freedom and watch it manifest itself right in front of our eyes. Happiness is felt on the inside, for that is where it lies. It is already in us. Set it free. To everything that tries to hold us back and hold us down, be resilient. For it does not define us, make us or break us. It only holds the potential to make us stronger.

Chapter VI

THROUGH THE MUD

There is this moment in the race that is going to determine whether you will podium, if you will have what it takes to cross the line with your hands in the air or whether you will go home disappointed. It is this specific moment where it hurts so bad. All of a sudden, your legs tighten, your mind grows weak, and you feel like you can't move. If you hold on and endure that pain for as long as it lasts, it will break free. In fact, you don't even have to ride the pain for long. You just have to hold long enough until the competition gives up and you break free. There were times that it literally lasted only for about five seconds and everyone fell behind. Something about competition, it is a zero-sum game. Seeing another person struggle gives you a weird sense of strength that somehow propels you to the trophy. It is my least favorite part of competition.

Many times, I have lost that battle. The last half mile, my legs feel like they are going to fall off. I give in. I am so close yet not near enough that I am forced to watch the winner cross the line as if I was a spectator. In order to overcome that, one must fight mentally, physically and emotionally. In essence, we must give everything in that moment, for it is going to determine the outcome of your endeavor.

It was Healthy Kidney 10k 2017, in New York City. We were running hard on the rolling hills in Central Park. Going into the last miles it was myself and three other guys. We were blasting. We must have been going 4:20 per mile pace. We could tell this was it. The moment was coming when the real race would begin. It wasn't long until Thomas Longosiwa, a bronze medalist for Kenya in the 2012 Olympics, jumped into the lead and turned up the pace. Teshome Mekonen fell off the group. I told myself, "This is it. You need to go for the podium. Get in there. Dig deep." I passed Mekonen and stayed up with Stephen Sambu.

Sambu and I are friends and I've trained with him before. He was the defending champion and I knew his capabilities. I thought if I could just stick with him, I'd be good. Longosiwa really seemed like he was dictating the race. I thought he might be on his way to winning it. I felt like Sambu and I were on the same team, fighting Longosiwa. The pace continued to get hotter. I felt myself dropping. I took a breath and as soon as I did, the gap between myself and the guys began to form. I settled and just hoped that Sambu could get Longosiwa. Just a few moments later though as I started to settle in my own rhythm, I could see Sambu dropping up ahead. There was less than a mile to go. I couldn't just sit back. I had to at least put up a fight.

I knew there was still some time. I decided to push. I chased forward until I passed Sambu and had Longosiwa within reach. I said to myself, "Look forward. Keep your form. Give 100 percent. Whatever happens, happens, as long as I go all out." With a total of 6.2 miles in the race, there was only that .2 left. I turned on my full lights. I just chased Longosiwa down with everything I had. I could see a turn ahead and I found myself on the left side, inside the turn. Next thing we knew, as soon as we made our way around the corner there was the home stretch. That one step brought me on the same page as Longosiwa. I looked down and kicked so hard. I went up this little hill and I could then see the finish tape. I couldn't see Longosiwa anymore. I had it. I pushed those last meters across the line and won that race with a huge smile. There were many times I wanted to give up. My body had had enough. My mind and heart though, were stronger and were able to tell my body to not surrender. It was a tough fight.

There are times in our life, where it is just like that. We face difficulties and hardships. To find our strength in them to endure, requires us to dig deep and realize there is more strength beneath the surface. Based on my experiences, I think that one must make the commitment to always persistently trust and adapt to the process. The rest will fall in its place. Believe that yes, you can do it and don't let doubt set in your head. What is the worst that can happen if you give everything? If you do, you will absolutely eliminate any doubts or what ifs. I have always found peace in giving everything. The peace comes when I give wholeheartedly regardless of the result.

The capability of the spirit is greater than that of our physical. We are stronger than we know. Our awareness is limited. I was helping my wife train for a local half marathon when we were living in Tucson, Arizona. I was riding with our son on the back of our bike and basically encouraging her through the miles. Around mile eight, I began to really push her. By her eleventh mile I sensed the weariness begin to set in. I could see her desire to slow and give into it. I coached her at that moment. Explaining that instead of giving up, she must push harder. It is now that you must realize that there is more energy than you can see. I knew she was going through that war of the mind. Her strides were being held back. Despite what one may think, the mental state was really what was limiting her more than the physical.

I did a similar run with my assistant coach in college. Derek Scott came to Liberty already a fast middle/long distance runner. He had just won a mile race and signed a contract with Puma. He was a good athlete. Scott always emphasized and made our team do core work after our run. We were supposed to meet on the field and spend at least twenty minutes doing core exercises, like crunches and leg lifts, as well as some stretches after our run. I was not enthusiastic about it.

I told him the reason I'm not into it is because the route I take on my run really crushes me. I didn't have much energy left and core was the last thing I wanted to do after. I believed that my route was the toughest, for anyone. It really was a challenging course. Evans Kigen and I thought we should give Scott a proper initiation to Lynchburg and have him go on the run with us. I didn't want to sugar coat it. It was going to be at least one hour and thirty minutes and tough. The most dangerous part was after thirty to forty minutes you hit a hill, and the hills continue to pop up around corners one after the next. You can't see beyond the hill you are on, until you are at the bottom of another. Those hills just keep coming.

Well, we took off. The run was going well until, just as I predicted, we started to hit those hills. He began to look at me. The harder the run became he would ask, "How much more?" I kept telling him, "Just a little further." I like to push up hills so he was really feeling it. He would ask, "Are we almost there?" I kept saying, "Yeah, this is the last one... Just one more." I knew if he knew how many there were, he would probably just want to jog it in. Finally, we hit the last one. When he got to the top, he could see the downhill. He knew he had done it. He told me later that he couldn't wait to call his girlfriend on the drive home. His head was hot, his body was wiped out, but at the end of the day he accomplished more than he thought he could. The run revealed to him a whole new level to his capability that he didn't know was possible. Derek told me that day was one of the things he remembers most about Lynchburg. The mind has to overcome the struggle ahead. There are limits beyond what you think you are capable.

There has to be a faith beyond what you can see. There is a purpose in the pain. We should not want to skip over that process. It is in that process that there is a sharpening and conditioning. We must be broken down to be built up stronger.

After a serious workout or a painful long run, many runners will seek out a mountainous runoff stream with water so cold it hurts. Others will go for the rivers in the north during the fall, oceans in the winter, or simply dump bags of ice into a bathtub. Going against every natural instinct, the runner will then get into the water waist deep. The first reaction my body always gives, no matter how many times I have done this, is to jump right back out. It starts out as shocking. Then the pain starts to kick in. My wife always laughs as she watches this process. It hurts so much. 'Why am I doing this?' I ask myself. Every time, like clockwork, around minute three, I say "That's it, I'm giving up." I forget why I'm doing it in the first place. It doesn't feel worth it. If I stay steady though, by minute four or five my body starts to go numb. Then I remember again the reason: the next day I will be fresher than today. This ice bath will heal my muscles and instigate a faster recovery. The pain has its purpose and it is for my good.

When you are in the thick of it, try to recognize its purpose. See beyond and embrace it. Reach for what is so close. Know the storm will end. The tunnel is almost at its end. It is how we hold that will make us. My good friend in college, Jordan Whitlock, and I liked to go off the grid for our training. One summer we sought out one of Colorado's highest peaks for our long run day. Mt. Elbert in Leadville, Colorado reaches 14,440 feet into the sky and to get there, one must cross rivers, rocks, steep inclines, and treacherous climbs. We ran straight for it, basically sprinting from the moment we entered the trail head. It wasn't long before our heads were soaked with sweat and our shoes soaked from crossing those creeks and rushing rivers. By the time we were closing in on the peak, we hit snow and altitude that had us frozen to the core and our lungs breathing tight. I left Jordan and made it to the top in a total time of one hour and five minutes. After a quick glance at the amazing view, I headed back down to find Jordan who I thought would've been right behind me.

I found him about a quarter of a mile down the mountain, slightly delirious and sitting on a large rock. "What are you doing Jordan? Let's go," I said, as I grabbed him by the arm and began pulling him to the summit. He had truly come to his edge. In his exhaustion, he had shut off any possibility of reaching the summit and he had concluded that the peak was just too far for him to reach. Little did he know he was almost there. He needed to go just a bit further. He had to hold on just a bit more. I found him in complete weariness and defeat on that rock. By the time we had reached the summit together though, once he could see the view and the heights that he just climbed, his despondency immediately turned to exhilaration. We took off our shirts, played in the snow, and posed for pictures, all the while laughing. For Jordan to think he was going to make it to the peak after he had made up his mind in defeat, seemed impossible. Once he made it though, he could see clearly not only the view, but the heights that one is able to climb if he can just believe and refuse to give up.

Paul Tergat taught me how to run in the mud. You have to glide. Your motion has to be swift. If you settle too much into each step then you too will sink in and your pace will slow. When one encounters trouble, tough times, struggle, pain, a tired spirit, a weariness, or a defeat, we must instigate the greatness within us. We must do so by seeing past the circumstances. Keep your pace swift and steady. Happiness cannot be dependent. It cannot get stuck in the mud. It must span beyond the surface. It must embrace every moment knowing its purpose. Most times the purpose is in the pain. Struggles, trials, tough times, and obstacles make us tougher and wiser in the end. We are never the same as we were once on the other side of it. We have to keep the faith and see the light in it. We have to understand that there is more than our eyes can see.

Chapter VII

CHIVALE

When I first started running in Kenya and had just joined that running group in Ngong Hills, I went out for my very first training run. I saw those pessimistic faces staring my way. It was hard to ignore them. Day after day seemed harder than the first. The runs were painful and difficult. I couldn't see how I could keep doing it. I didn't show any signs of significant improvement. When I felt the hurt, when I thought too much about it, it only made sense to give up. "These guys know what they are talking about. I don't have what it takes."

Our minds amplify the negative and our hearts soak it up like a sponge. I was in last place during those days. We would go out for a run as a large group and I would be seen running behind all the rest trying to catch them like I had brought a knife to a gun fight. Better yet it felt like I had brought a stick to a gun fight. I wasn't even in the same boxing ring. I was so far behind one day, that I couldn't see anyone in front of me and made a wrong turn forcing me to come back hours later. I had a decision to make. I was at a crossroads. Was the prize ahead of me really worth pushing toward? Was it worth chasing knowing my chance of survival was feeble?

I remembered the words Paul told me. "Just finish the program." He was encouraging me to not worry about pace or position, but to just finish the miles. I would tell myself again and again, "Just keep going." As soon as I committed to not giving up on it and run my own race, it all changed. I can picture one run so clearly now. We took off as usual and I was in the back just like every other day. As I made the turn that runs over a hill overlooking the town center, I could see one guy, Chivale. He was running within eyesight and within reach. He was about 200 meters away. The dirt roads that we ran on had many short turns. I realized I wasn't the only one in the back. I wasn't alone in the struggle. When I felt like I was in the trenches, I realized I wasn't the only one there. I said to myself, just catch up with Chivale and work with him. So, I did. That was the moment that really propelled me into the next chapter of my running.

Chivale and I worked together and the following day we decided to try and catch the next guy running just ahead of us. We caught him and I kept on pushing. Every run I would aim to get just a little closer to the pack ahead of me. Of course, it wasn't easy, but the process was exciting. I pushed and pushed until I was with the elite lead pack. One particular hill always proved to be problematic for me. I cannot tell you how many times I got dropped at that very same spot. Like clockwork I would reach the base of the hill and on my way to the top of it I would choke up from its steepness. Eventually though, I had pushed so hard and accelerated so fast over it that when I caught up to Paul in the front, he looked at me and said, "Young man get back. You are not ready to be here." Well, he was slightly right since after a few weeks of me running with those top guys, I suffered shin splints that lasted a couple months. In the long run, I had made it.

I picture myself in those first days of running like a strong body of water that was being held back by a dam. It was just waiting to rush and flow at incredible speed and power. One must release their own dam of doubt and fear and every thought holding themselves back in captivity. Previously there were voices that I listened to that said, "You're a nobody." If you listen closely though, you can hear "You can do it. You have what it takes." The most important voice was mine. I had grown to believe and could then say, "I can" and "I will." Confidence, motivation, determination and drive come from within. No one knows what is in store for you. Listen to the right people. Connect with the right people. Most importantly, believe. Find your hope and fight for it.

Guard against stifling the flame. Have you ever watched a fire and seen how the flame grows stronger when it has a branch to reach for? To not doubt why, but have confidence that whatever happens, it is for the good. You may wonder why you are here in this situation, in this place, in these circumstances, and where you are going? Not only can one not change what already has been, but one cannot even dream to think he has the ability to foresee the hypothetical past. Look forward with confidence. The footprints that you now leave behind were set before you ahead of time. All can understand that not one man on earth has full control of their outcomes, but can all grasp the idea that the attempt to try to do so is also useless? It doesn't have to be easy; it just has to be right. Life is just that, life. What we make of it is what makes the difference.

2016 Olympic Trials in Eugene, Oregon the athletes lined up like stallions ready to slay. We were about to be thrust into that stadium like gladiators. Each one given a sword and they say fight. Now all of the sudden the same track that I had run so many events and practices on, was different. I looked at the stadium full to the brim with spectators, agents, coaches, sponsors and cameras, yet it felt so empty. It was as if I was watching as a bird flying high in the sky looking down upon it all. The Olympic Trials were the epitome of track and field. This was it. Every four years the big stage comes and this was that time. All of the key players were there, each one wanting that ticket. They've been training for months. God only knows what each one of them had gone through to get there.

Since 2008 I had wanted to represent the USA and wear that racing singlet with the red, white, and blue.

Eight years later I got my chance to run in the 10,000m trials. My stomach was filled with so many butterflies. I had to find a trash can to throw up in while I was making my way to the start area. I began to doubt my preparation. It felt like eight years hadn't been enough time to get ready. We took to the line with temperatures in the nineties. I remember while the announcer gave the introductions of the athletes, I thought my body was already exhausted. I just wanted to go sit in the shade somewhere. The sun beat down and my veins were already giving in before we had even started.

Then the gun went off whether I was ready or not. I couldn't keep up with the pace. I felt immediately drained. The lead pack took off and all I could think was how overheated I felt. I didn't feel the fire. I just said to myself, "Just hang the best you can." As I saw the gaps opening and my defeat ahead of me, I just told myself, "This is your job and give it everything nonetheless." Although it was not my day, nor the circumstances I thought it would be, I decided to just work. I resolved to keep the faith and just finish the program as Paul told me back in the day. I grabbed cold water at the tables they had set up along the track and ran through all of the hoses that were held up to spray and cool the runners. I thought I might legitimately pass out. I remember halfway through thinking, "Wow, is this it? All of this build up has led to this?" I never imagined such a sloppy defeat for my most important race. I couldn't even handle the pace.

Something happened though. Just as I mentally settled and accepted defeat, the guys in the front pack started slowing, some even dropping off. The leaders were feeling the heat of it all just as I was. The pace began to slow. I couldn't believe it. Some of the guys who took off at the beginning, I now saw laying on the side of the track in exhaustion. Some were walking off as I passed them. I looked ahead and saw more runners starting to crash. I wasn't the only one feeling it. It was as if I was seeing Chivale back in Kenya all over again. It was a beacon of hope. I just needed to stay strong and hang on.

At that point, Olympics wasn't even in my mind. I just thought, "Just finish your job." Sometimes you're in a struggle and it may no longer even be about what it was to start with. It's just about taking a breath and making it through the next moment, the next hour. As I kept plugging along, I started to catch up. I just fought. I kept fighting. Before I knew it, there was one lap to go. The finish line had arrived. I crossed the line in sixth place overall. It was amazing to me, for when we started and through the thick of the race, it looked like I was going to be in last or twentieth place. I remember the officials coming to me, handing me a card as I walked from the finish line and them telling me I will need to process for the Olympic team. I said, "I think there has been a mistake."

They said, "No, you are the fourth guy with the qualifying time, you are the alternate for the Olympic team." I remember holding that paper saying, "Wow." It meant something to me. I thought I had run the worst race of my life. I felt helpless, yet I walked away with a token that gave me something out of it. It was a reminder that the fight was worth it. I fought my own fight that day. It wasn't about the race itself; it was the journey I took at Hayward Field that day that had me walking away feeling like I had won. When I least expected it, when all odds were against me, I was being held on. I was given just enough to keep me going. In the end we don't need any medal, what we do need though will always be there to see if we can find it in ourselves. Although I was rewarded with the chance of going to the Olympics, my real profit was found in the process.

Chapter VIII

UNDER THE SUN

The concepts we knew as children, still remain the same today. All that has changed is the way in which we accept and see them. I believe the race to happiness is not going to be achieved by seeking it out as the finish line. We each must seek love and truth. That is when we will be led to happiness. The harder one searches in the wrong places, they soon find themselves in a quickly deepening hole. Happiness is not something one may hold or even see; it is a state of mind and heart. You don't have to think about it, it happens. The most high and lofty person struggles to find it the same as the lowliest person (according to worldly standards). What will make the difference is one's ability to see and taste truth. Life isn't about the top of that mountain peak, but about the journey to the destination. How will we walk this road we are on? The rain comes down on us all. The sun shines on us all in the same way.

One of my greatest struggles as an elite runner arose when I felt pride start to rub off on me. I would look around and start to embrace the vanity of being a fast, elite runner. I would run with someone on the trails for months and see them as my fellow teammate. When I would return from having achieved something great, or having received some title, I would find I was then treated differently. There was a temptation to hold myself differently as well. It was as if my status had changed then and there. How could a race change a man from within? How could a title alter the man himself, in just one weekend? It was that power of status again, this time in the form of a medal one wore around the neck.

A book in the Bible often refers to what is done under the sun. It is a beautiful way at looking at life. The sun has been and will always be the same. It has risen and set time and time again over generation after generation. The book argues that truly nothing new can be done under the sun. Man has already done it all. The realization we must come to is to understand that what we become, our acts, our goods, everything on this earth that is earthly will all amount to nothing more than it already has. It is the wind one's actions bring, the heart that grows with every step, the difference one makes in the life of another, the understanding one gains, the vision that grows and widens with our steps that mean something. It is what the journey brought to life under the sun.

We have to see beyond. Get to the root of where our human existence begins, and we must stay there. We are all human beings. We all need water and air to survive and we all have a heart that beats for love.

There was a crisis in Kenya in 2007. It was a political crisis at the source of it. What began as corruption in the government led to a widespread tribal conflict. It started when President Mwai Kibaki was thought to have rigged his reelection. This sent the supporters of his opponent, Raila Odinga, in an uprising. There quickly grew a time of violence and killing. The most targeted people were the Kikuyu tribe. People would come and burn the Kikuyu homes with families still inside.

I heard a story from a friend that is worth retelling. His family lived on a beautiful piece of farmland in the Rift Valley. They had wonderful neighbors. They were good friends for a long time. They often shared crops and harvests as well as helped each other when in need. They spent some afternoons sharing tea and watching their children play together. In 2007, when the crisis came, it reached all the way toward their town. My friend's family heard word that the uprising was planning to come and burn their neighbors' house the next day. Even though their neighbors were Kikuyu, they were still the people they had loved all of those years. They knew their hearts.

How could they ever imagine hating them to the point of burning them? It was unfathomable. They knew their very being was beyond any tribal affiliation. Their blood ran the same. So, in the night they secretly told their neighbors of the tragedy that would strike the next day. They told them to pack up and leave with no one seeing them. They would then set fire to their home early the next morning so the opposition would think their home was already reached and would not know that they were given secret word.

Nothing was truly different between those two families, except maybe the accent on their tongue and possibly a few facial features. To try to say somehow their tribal association made them innately different is nonsensical. What man can judge is what he can see. Therefore, he cannot judge another's heart but only the evidence of what flows from it. May we examine the veins that run and see truth in it all. We all bleed the same blood. We are all on the same search. May we see the heart of man.

The man I once was cannot be judged differently now just based on my achievements, class, status, money, and fame. Yet, this is what I have experienced. When I was a child, our family was looked down upon, ridiculed, ignored, even despised at times, simply because we had less than others. We were considered the poorest of the poor. One would think there would be mercy, for the people looking down on us knew too what it felt like to have little. That was not the case though. We were outcasts.

I remember scraping porridge from the bottom of the pot grasping for every last drop. I remember the days I snuck a small milk carton that the school gave out to the students once a month into my bag beside my desk.

I would later bestow it upon my mom and see her sigh of gratitude for she could then use it to make tea for our family. There were days I would sprint home along that rocky path during lunchtime. I would be so eager to see what my sister had cooked, only to find that there was no food for lunch that day. I would then run along that rocky path right back to school. I was never sad for I knew we would have enough when we needed it. I was embarrassed though. For I saw the faces that stared upon our family. I could feel their eyes like daggers.

We may not have had kerosene to light our lamps at night. We may have had only tomatoes for lunch that Christmas day, but I never saw us as less. I felt like others did, though. Now, with the same skin, the same voice, the same character, I am elevated. I am looked up to and admired. I am sought out as a friend and someone wished to be connected with. Why? Is it possible that it is because my status has changed? I fear it is true. My tribe, my medals, what one can see about me cannot be what defines me. My soul is the same as it was when I delivered milk on my brother's bike. I am the same man now as I was when I was tending to my cows and leading them from the woods to the river for a drink.

I was Sam then, and I am Sam now. My achievements can be found in storage boxes in the corner of our garage. They mean nothing more than a part of my journey. The parties I've attended, the fancy meals, bright lights, pay checks, cars parked in my driveway, shouldn't define me. They should in no way alter how one sees me. I've been to the top and I've been to the bottom. I am the same man. My heart still pumps the same blood. Whether I wore shoes made from old scraps of tires or the latest Nike innovated shoe design before it was even released to the public, I am Sam. My innermost being may have learned, grown, and felt, but nothing ever seen from the outside ever changed who I am. Therefore, it is nonsensical to attempt to strive for any of those things described, in hopes that it will fill any vacancy of the heart. It can fill only temporarily, conditionally, and only reach the shallows. It will not reach the depths of our soul. It cannot change your innermost being, at least not for the good.

If one could take away just one thing from this book may it be that. We all have a heart. May we see one another in the same light. Have mercy, for the rain falls and the sun shines on us all. The man lays beneath it all.

Chapter IX

TO SEE THE HEART

It was the spring of 2017 in Kampala, Uganda. The grassy field was before me. The stadium was overflowing with faces just waiting in watch for the race to start. The afternoon sun was beating down on us and the humidity and altitude didn't help. I had been in Uganda for two and a half days, but was still feeling the jet lag. As we rode on a bus from our hotel to Kololo Stadium, I took time to soak in the sights and significance of the race ahead of me. This was going to be the biggest race of my career to date. Uganda is a lot like Kenya and being in Kampala reminded me of my childhood. My heart was at peace as I entered the field to get ready for battle. I could see the finishing banner across the way between a couple of palm trees. I knew the race that was ahead of me would be long and trying. It felt like there was a mountain between me and that moment where I could cross under that banner.

I had walked away from the USATF Cross Country Championships in Bend, Oregon with a fourth-place finish and a ticket to represent the US and compete against the world's best cross-country runners in Uganda. So, there I stood, lacing up my spikes, wearing the USA uniform, and about to run in the World Cross Country Championships in Kampala.

As we took the line, I still had no idea what was in store. It was still hot and the sun was beating down even harder. I looked around me and all I could see was a sea of incredible competition. To my left and my right was runner after runner of extreme capability. I felt like a speck among it all. The racecourse was built to have the men race a two-kilometer loop six times. My teammates and I had high hopes of placing top three as a team. We positioned ourselves on the line. Shadrack Kipchirchir and Stanley Kebenei were going to lead and then Lenny

Korir, Scott Fauble and I were going to follow. Since I was fourth coming in, I planned to start conservatively for the first couple of laps. My goal was to do everything possible to score points for team USA. Our team head coach was Ed Eyestone, a man of great respect. He had gone over every scenario with us in order to try and estimate where we would be as individuals and as a team. Based on his stats, he had me believe I could score big points if I raced smart. He told us that he would yell our positions to us each lap we passed by him to allow us to know where we were among the big field.

When then gun went off, I just kept steady and focused on what was in front of me. It was useless to try to position myself or gain any ground among all of the fast runners during the first lap. The pace I was going was so tough that I was ready to be done after the first lap. Sweat was pouring off my face. I wiped my eyes continuously in an attempt to keep the salt out. It was a race of heart. By the second lap of the course it was starting to string out a bit. I was feeling the heat even more.

As I neared the corner of the second turn though, I heard someone shouting at me to my right. It was Lydia, Damaris and Egla! My sisters had made the journey from their homes in Kenya to see me race. They shouted so loud I could hear them amongst all the noise. It gives me chills even now thinking about it. I was running for them. I have been running all these years for them and was never able to show them firsthand. Here they were though, cheering me on. It felt as though it finally came full circle. I got the boost I needed. I trekked forward on the course. I felt like I was home. I immediately felt like the dirt in front of me was just as the dirt I felt under my bare feet in the village.

I fought the inclination to give in to the exhaustion. I knew I had to give everything, despite the fact that my chances of winning felt so far out of reach. Even though I was so far behind the leaders, I just kept running. I know at one point I was in twenty-sixth place. I had no idea where my team was or where I stood in line of everyone, but I just kept running as hard as I could. I saw coach at one point yelling and shouting, "You're in top fifteen!" All I knew was with every effort I used to drive forward I would somehow gain leverage and pass a few more runners. It was most certainly one of the hottest races of my life. Not only was the temperature hot, but the competition even more so. The racers were fierce and tough.

The high altitude was intimidating and trying. I could see we were on the last lap of the course. I pushed one last time. My body was at its limits. I crossed the line having no idea what place I was in. I was rewarded when I saw the leaderboard. After a long and trying race, I was proud to see my eleventh-place finish. I was the first American to cross the line.

I was so excited and relieved. After cooling down and soaking it all in, I posted a photo on twitter in my excitement. I wrote, "I wouldn't recommend racing in Africa. Super thankful for eleventh place overall." I just kept thinking I didn't know how that was possible. The race was so hard with all of the amazing competition. By the time I landed back in America though, I had received so many twitter and private messages, voicemails, and emails all regarding that now viral tweet.

Somehow my sarcasm was lost in translation. Instead of what I thought was just a simple social media post to say thank you and to show my appreciation for a great day in Uganda, I was bombarded by negativity and hate. It was hard for me to fathom that people would read that tweet and think I would insult the race and Africa. What I meant, wasn't what some people perceived. In reality, I loved my time in Uganda and was trying to compliment what was a hard-fought race. What I learned from this experience is that, despite the best of intentions, people may still misperceive and come to judge and hate. I realized the only thing that could bring peace in the situation was to know that God sees the heart and we are called to love.

I had to let it go and realize that it was just a misunderstanding. I needed to try to see beyond it all. Carrie Tollefson, in a pre-race interview before the Healthy Kidney 10k that was about two weeks after the tweet, asked me if I wanted to talk on the situation. I told her I had been thinking back to Martin Luther King and that his words kept resonating in my heart. Ultimately, God sees your heart. If someone hurts you, love them back. If you see something you don't like, shine light on it. We may sit on opposite ends of the table at the meeting, but may we see beyond the papers spread across it and see the man on the other side.

Chapter X

SIMPLICITY

The school bell rang and all the children, including myself, made that daily run home for lunch. I ran down that rocky dirt path full of joy. There was a peace in the life we were living. We were children. There wasn't much to think about except school and chores. As I made that run home though I had a high suspicion there wasn't going to be much for lunch that day. During that time in my life it was just myself, my sister Janet and my dad at the homestead. Usually, if there was going to be lunch, the night before my sister and I would boil corn and beans so that the next day we would just sauté them with some onions from the garden. The night before though, there were no corn and beans to boil.

When I arrived home, my suspicions came to be true. I resorted to the lemon tree that was my friend every once in a while. That tree and I were bitter friends. When my stomach was hungry and my lips parched, I made that climb up. I can picture myself now with my body dangling from the branch as I reached for the lemon above me. The thorns on the tree were grinning at me in wait to poke my hand as I got closer to the fruit. With just a few scrapes, I was able to loosen the lemon from the branch and enjoy the sweet nectar.

Though bitter to most who do not partake of it often, when one is hungry and thirsty enough, there is a beauty in how delicious it really is. Although it is a short tree, full of thorns, and the lemon is bitter, it kept me going that day. I sat in the dry grass under that tree peeling and biting that sour fruit. One cannot help but see that although it is not always pretty, in life if you have faith, you will have just what you need to hold.

Our homestead was made up of two mud huts and a small grass thatched granary storage. It overlooked a great valley below full of green. The Kaberasel village lay in a mountainous region. It is not quite like what you see on TV and in magazines depicting Kenya. My village is far from those areas. Kabarasel is cold at nights and rainy some days. The woods are thick, the trails windy, and most of all, it is hilly. Our farm is found on top of a hill behind a wooden fence my dad made years ago. It then spans down the valley across two rolling hills. We grew mainly corn, though we had beans, potatoes, and yucca growing as well.

As I sat in the grass, I could see the land that my cousin and I had just finished plowing. I was proud and knew my mom would have been proud to see all of the soil we had dug and made ready for planting. I sat planning the logistics for the potatoes I would plant in the coming weeks and the beans that we would soon be able to harvest and boil. I was looking at the corn that would be dry soon and ready to be husked and ground into grain for ugali. Ugali is a staple food in Kenya. It is eaten by most for dinner. It looks like a cake of grits. It is delicious and goes well with milk, stew, or greens. I always joke to my friends that we would never hear the question, "What do you want for dinner?" In my life as a kid, Ugali was always what was for dinner, every day.

We literally lived off the land. We were living that simple life. That little piece of ground would provide so much for me and my family. It was much different than what I am used to now. It taught me humility of nature. We were to be stewards to the soil that kept giving to us. Part of it reminds me of the ways the generations before me lived and how they did it. I can see how that simplicity is needed in the modern life. I find myself looking at a loaf of bread thinking, "Wow, we didn't even know how to make bread in the village back then, let alone see it prepackaged in a bag that we can buy at any convenience store."

It is easy to lose our tether to reality nowadays. We must force our minds into gratitude. From that standpoint we can see how it comes down to the bread that gives us life. We must appreciate all of the little parts. We as people tend to focus on the deficiencies or what we are lacking. If we are able to turn our attention on what we do have and what we can be grateful for, we will find life becomes much simpler.

There is beauty in seeing that simplicity in life. Finding one's place in the small things. In order to find joy anywhere else, one must first be able to find it at home.

There is a saying I have heard many times from people in the village. They say, "Go where there are stars during the day." I think one can interpret that saying in many different ways. I like to use it to remind myself to see the stars that shine in the everyday. They are sometimes hard to see, but if one looks closely, he will see stars shining all around him to admire and stare at with wonder.

If only we could see the beauty and truth in how blessed we already are. When we are able to stop searching and striving so hard, we can find life becomes much simpler, and happier. My cousin Ben had a cow. It was notorious for always looking really big and full. What most didn't know though, was that Ben wanted his cow to look that way. Instead of working hard and being a good shepherd, bringing his cows to the fields to graze and fill up on food, Ben found another way. He would sprinkle salt into the cow's water so it would drink more. The cow wasn't really as full as it appeared, it was really just bloated up on water. There are opportunities to bloat up on just about anything in this life. We drink in waters that only appear to make us stronger and don't truly satisfy. I've found that if one can stop filling up on the wrong things, he will find a simple yet satisfying life.

Chapter XI

WHAT IS SUCCESS?

Imagine that you have been on pursuit of a hefty treasure for quite some time now. Then all of a sudden, your journey leads you to a mountainside tunnel. You learn that a truck transporting radioactive materials crashed on the other side of it and now the tunnel is filled with active radiation. You are left with no other option but to take the tunnel and score the treasure or turn back empty-handed. If you do decide to enter the tunnel though, you will be exposed to massive radiation that is guaranteed to kill you in due time, but you will have all the treasure, fame and all that money can buy.

Would you push through or would you turn back to tell the story of the journey that got you there?

Success is so sought out that the consequences can seem irrelevant. Could the end result really be worth the cost? Is it truly going to fulfill as hoped? The man will remain the same even after the gold. He will then find the need for another. He will find that the vanity never ends. Excessive pride does in fact lead down a road of futility. We need to consider that which we are chasing after. If it is out of the motivation to build up one's pride, I would argue that he will most likely find the end result to be as a mirage. The closer he gets to the prize he will see it fades with the background and vanishes as he reaches out to touch it. The convection of air rising up from the hot tar plays games with the eyes as do the motivations built on self.

They are desires with short term results. Like surfing on a crashing wave, once obtained, it eventually loses momentum and after it is gone another one must be found. We must leave no open crevices or gaps so that we may stay whole and not so easily deceived. The alternative will only leave us open to that which leads us away to the temporary, conditional, and the like. The end result will not fulfill as one had thought. Whether it is desperation or aspiration, our hearts will always long for something. To find one's mind idle is a very rare time. If achieved, it was most likely done intentionally.

I will cross the line of a big race with hands in the air. I will walk away with the medal and the prize. The plane ride home though, is spent with thoughts just planning the next race. I have had the fame, lights, money, trophies, and success yet there is always another race to be run. May we not be racing toward an ever-retreating peak.

My son had a science experiment in school where he had to place a tea bag into a glass of water. The lesson stuck with me. As the crystal-clear water begins to become saturated by the tea, the color slowly changes. The longer the tea bag steeps, the darker the color changes. This is of course a simple concept, but one must ponder the idea that the darker the water becomes, it is harder to see the clarity it once had. We become so used to that which is around us. We see everyone chasing, so shouldn't we be chasing also? We see the margins that are set around us, so shouldn't we too be living to those standards as well? Just because it is the color of our tea does not mean it is how it should be. We must strive to see through the taint and into the clarity.

May mediocrity and rationalization not dictate our steps. Instead, may we surrender our fight. There is this temptation to chase, to build, to create, to make a name for oneself, to achieve, to put one's name on something, to be validated, to be accepted, and most of all to assemble a persona to be seen and looked up to. In order to chase the things we believe will help us succeed, we have to fight for it. Using all sorts of tactics, we strive to make success, to make our happiness. This will always lead to failure. Have you ever pondered the idea that anything of this world requires some degree of selfishness and anything of the heart requires selflessness?

I had to incur three injuries before I came to the realization of the need to slow down, let it be, and appreciate what already was. I chased those races. I broke my fourth metatarsal in my left foot after having beaten down the laps on the track in the spring of 2013. I missed a whole summer of training and spent it feeling sorry for myself. I was angry, disappointed, and aggravated that I had trained so hard and it led only to having to miss all the races I had been preparing for. I got healthy again and about six months later I ran that epic race, where I ran 13:04 in the indoor 5,000 meters. I got excited and hit those miles and laps around the track again. Down I went again with another metatarsal. Instead of coming to my senses and seeing the purpose in the injuries, I only resorted to fighting and refusing to accept it. I spent my days in recovery mad and disappointed. So, the cycle came again. I recovered and ran 13:16 that summer in Berlin. I then went straight back at the miles again.

Though I was thankful to be back at it, I missed the opportunity to appreciate when I was down. It was as if I was searching only for the highs. I could not find happiness when I was injured. I knew I needed to be healthy and that was that. I kept thinking, "I don't deserve this. Why me?" So, I kept grinding those miles, having not changed my heart at all. Again, I incurred a stress fracture in the same foot. I was in Tucson, Az when I injured my foot for the last time. I was finally able to get clarity. I found there was no use in fighting. It was the cost of doing this running business and running miles and miles at speeds inconceivable. A great friend once told me that the time you are most susceptible to failure is when everything seems to be going well and you don't see it coming. The best times for learning are when one is down. It is in the trials, that one is able to grow. I had to incur three rough running injuries and setbacks in my training before I could finally see the point.

My story isn't about how far and fast I've come. My story is found in the journey. As I was laid up on the couch, in my boot, I had blessings all around me. I could turn to any direction and find more than one thing to be thankful for. I came home that day from the X-ray exam in Tucson, driving down the road surrounded by cacti, nothing but blue in the sky, and the hot desert air coming through the windows. I wasn't sure what to do next. What would we do? I couldn't race, yet again. What would Nike say? How would I make any extra cash without being able to run those road races? How long would this injury take to heal? All reasonings were against me. I turned back to the desert air. I breathed in and looked forward. I quieted my mind and reflected on the now. There I was, driving home to my wife and son. I realized I had already won. My mind had been so busy chasing and running, I was unable to rest in what already was. I focused on the hot black tar road in front of me as I drove, and my anger left me. I was at peace with the circumstances.

The beauty in life is that all we have to do is show up. Then we get to watch how it unravels and where it goes. You will have a win when and if it is your time. My coach in college, Brant Tolsma, used to tell me, "It's fine to be successful. What you really want is to be successful in the right things." In college, coach Tolsma used to do things so simple. I was warming up before the South East Regionals in North Carolina. It was ninety degrees out. He came up and said, "Ignore me, I'm just putting ice behind your head. Now give me your wrist. This will help cool you." He would look at my spike. I'd ask, "What is the plan?" He'd smile and say, "Why are you asking me? You already know." He believed in me. He'd say, "Go do your thing. I don't doubt you." During practice he would listen when I said I was tired. He would laugh and say, "Wow, I guess you're human after all." "I'm glad you are tired. It makes sense. You are putting in the work." Our longest conversations while traveling on those long bus rides and long plane layovers, would be either regarding faith or jokes.

Life can feel like we are driving a semi-truck up a steep hill in a light gear. One must ascend in the right gear. It isn't until one shifts that he will make it to the top with ease. Not everything ends with winning or losing a race. May we not miss the point. We are toeing a line that we have already won.

Chapter XII

THE CALL TO SERVE

This is the most important chapter of this book. All the stories I have shared up until now, have been about the focus on how to harness the strength within us. Now I want to shift and focus on how we can be so full, that pouring ourselves out onto others is the only step left to take. What is a steward? I think that the greatest achievement that anyone can have is to be able to say that they lived a life not just for self, but also for others. Often, when we think about giving, we think material. I think of the giving in absence of the material, that which requires our time, our efforts, our wishing of good will on others and even simply looking at our neighbors in good faith.

However, giving sometimes is not easy. In fact, there are times that it feels extremely difficult and without sense. Some people may even advise against your helping hand. Insisting that in some way your efforts are worthless, and that you surely cannot make a tangible difference. They may try to bloat you and feed you the idea that you matter more than those you are trying to help. What we must remember is that each moment, each person, every encounter, all opportunities that arise, are a chance to outpour the goodness from within. It is a chance to make the life we are living count for good outside of ourselves. There is a Swahili saying that goes, "Tenda mema, Enda zako." Translation; do good and go your way. Meaning, all you have to do is do good and the rest will take care of itself. If one is able to serve, whether it requires much or little of oneself, he will know he is where he is supposed to be. He does not need to see the result or even feel the gratitude from the other side. The satisfaction comes from knowing there is no other place and time than the present to value another more than self.

Deep in the woods at Fort Jackson, South Carolina, Captain Rose approached me. "Trainee! You have phone call." I was without words. I hadn't spoken on the phone in months. I hadn't heard any music other than the cadences sung by myself and my fellow soldiers since the day I was dropped off from the bus early that first morning. I hadn't seen my children for countless nights, except in the photos I stared at before I went down to rest on my military bunk. It had been too long, and I had been growing weary. I missed my family. Who would it be on the phone? I wondered if I was in trouble or what was going to be asked of me.

I took the phone and as Drill Sergeant Jefferson stood over me, I put it to my ear. It was my wife! Deep in the woods of South Carolina I heard the voice of my wife. I had only been reading her thoughts through the letters we exchanged for the last three months. Her voice felt like honey. To explain how I felt at that moment is difficult to describe. Basic training was difficult both mentally and physically. More than any difficulty I faced there though, none compared to missing my family. After a very quick hello though, I had to think why. Why was I receiving this phone call in the middle of the woods? I would then learn the reason, and it was crazy.

ABC 20/20 was doing an episode called the <u>Real Rookies</u> to prequel and promote a new show series called the Rookie. It was about a man who at a later age in his life decided to change it all and switch careers to become a NYC police officer. Somehow, they had heard that I too was switching careers later in my life and they wanted to feature my story.

My wife had been contacted and she was asked to be interviewed and our family to be filmed for a day. She was calling to make sure this was all okay with me. I can't imagine being my wife. She hadn't seen me or heard my voice since the day I left for boot camp. Then as she was going to pick up our oldest son from school, she received a phone call from a Lieutenant Colonel telling her she has been requested to be on national television to be aired after Dancing with the Stars. I knew people would think it was bizarre, me leaving my lucrative professional athletic career to join the Army. Never would I have thought though, that my story would catch the attention of national television.

Many people do ask me that question of why? Why would I leave running at the peak of my career to join the Army? The answer to that lies in the same reason I wrote this book. What makes sense to the world does not always make sense to the soul. Our pastor once told us, "See with your heart and not with your eyes." There is a road to happiness and it is not found by chasing self-fulfillment. We have a purpose much beyond ourselves. The more we look outside, the more we will fill the inside. Running can fill as long as one is running for the right reason. I had come to a point in my running though, that I could no longer see that reason. I found myself chasing after a line that I no longer felt was worth crossing. I could no longer see the value in the gold. I knew I had finished that chapter in my journey. I knew I had a new call.

I sit here now with a M240B machine gun laying across the table in front of me. It is four AM and we are about to set off for a day in the woods at Fort Pickett, Virginia for another day of Officer training. I would never have imagined myself in this position. I would never have thought I'd be carrying an eighty-pound ruck on my back with all the supplies needed to spend a week in the woods training to be a Quartermaster Army Officer. That was my call though. The Army was the answer for me. To serve our country and our fellow man. To dig deep and give everything alongside other men and women who are already in service. Though it seems bizarre to another, to me I knew it made all the sense in the world. If we are using a map to find happiness we are already lost. If we have a graph or a chart, it is useless.

I have met many men who have found that truth. That truth that goes against everything the world tries to tell us. The reason one would rather go without, so another man could go with. The way one can smile because they brought a smile to someone else. How one's heart can be full because another is filled. I was on the receiving end of that feet washing in 2009.

I was at Liberty and the track team was going on a mission trip to Ngong Hills, Kenya. A very kind man, Dan Newell, felt called to donate some money to the track team and without even knowing it, he kindly sponsored me to go along. We were working at a local middle school there in Ngong and our track team was preparing their dirt track for an upcoming meet we were going to host for the local school kids. When it was time to leave for the day, some of the guys decided to run back to the ostrich farm where we were staying. I was riding on the bus alongside the guys running and I could see this man in the distance running so slow. He was trying to keep up with the college kids. I had no idea who he was, but I thought that I had better go keep him company so he doesn't get eaten by a lion or something. Of course, I was kidding about the lion, but I jumped off the bus nonetheless.

I said, "Hey how's it going?" He answered, "Good, just trying to see if these old legs can still hang." Jay and I had an instant connection. He told me he was from Colorado. We ended up talking the whole time on that long run back to the farm. He told me all about his life and we ended up talking about some deep stuff in our lives. We realized we both had experienced a great loss of a loved one. Jay shared with me that he had just lost his son and his wife was really hurting from the grief. I told him I had lost my mother when I was young. We both felt the desire to connect. Jay and his wife Shari never left my life since that day. That run with Jay is a time I will never forget. You never know the people that will come into our lives and the way we can impact one another.

Jay is such a fun guy. He still works full time raising lambs for a living. He also runs marathons in his late fifties. I once jokingly told him that he was the slowest person I knew because he finished in the 26,000 range in the New York City marathon. He and Shari have lots of fun together. They go on trips all over the country meeting all sorts of people. They truly know how to make the best of every moment. What I admire most about Jay though is his desire to give. For as much as that man has, he gives double. Though Jay was hurting from the loss of his son, he did not seek self. He did not resort to pity, to defeat, to anything of self. He got on a plane and went to help his friend build a rescue center for girls in Kenya. What drives a man to give? I have met millionaires who won't spare a dime. Yet, Jay sacrifices not only money, but time as well. He does not care where, when, or how far he has to go. If he sees a need, he would be happy to lend a hand.

There is something to giving. It is fulfilling. It feeds a part of us. It is that selfless part. It feeds our happiness because it is not feeding our bellies, but our souls. I ran mile after mile chasing a finish line that my feet would never reach.

That is why I found myself in the summer of 2018 looking for a way to change it all. I was tired of chasing after the wind. I wanted a place where I could make a difference. I could find joy in knowing my efforts would serve our country and our fellow man. When I found myself at basic training with a Drill Sergeant yelling in my ear while my hands held up a thirty-pound bag above my head for almost an hour, I knew I was there for a reason. Right then and there I was learning firsthand a valuable lesson of life. What makes me any different than the man to my right or left? All of my accolades, my earnings, medals, honors, and fame were thrown out the window at that very moment. We got straight to the root of man on the asphalt that day. As the summer sun beat down on our heads and the sweat poured down our face in Fort Jackson, South Carolina, I could see I was with the wind.

AFTERWORD

I hesitated in typing this last story as it was something I have always shut out and never wanted to talk about. I don't know why exactly, but to the best of my knowledge, I can say that it scares me a little. It might come to shock you, but I haven't told it to anyone, including my wife, until now. I have had great and tough times. This story fits neither of those. So here goes nothing.

About a year or so after I started running in Ngong Hills with Paul's group, I would start to feel a bit dizzy for the first ten or fifteen minutes of my morning runs and then it would go away. I thought it was just normal to feel that way especially when you're running a lot of hard miles. My body was still adapting to the tough training in those days and I couldn't tell if I was lacking something or if it was because of the intensity of long-distance running. I was staying with my cousin William in those days and I ran with him every day from his apartment to the point where we would start our long runs.

One morning, I was jogging with William along the same path that we took every morning and all of a sudden, I started to feel dizzy again and began to stumble. All I remember was yelling at William that I was feeling dizzy and losing my balance. The next thing I remember was that I woke up and all I could see was a glimmer of light and people around me with someone holding me. I was in a car or a pickup truck, or something. Before I could make any sense of it, I blacked out again.

Later that day, I woke up again, but in a hospital that I can't quite remember. My sister-in-law Lorna was looking back at me and she later told me that I was lucky to be alive. I had an IV tube connected to my arm and she said that I was low on blood sugar and dehydrated. Miraculously, I survived something that according to her was crazy. My cousin never wanted to tell me what happened and neither did I want him too. Since that day in 2005, I have never wanted to talk about it because it reminds me of the day that I don't know what happened to me. It was a time that I came face to face with my lack of control in life and how small I really am.

Overtime, I have come to learn and guess that I possibly passed out because of low blood sugar. I tend not to eat much when I am training hard. I think my body has adapted to going with so little in the tank. When training and running a lot of miles though, it needs more. I have since felt lightheaded a number of times, but I could easily fix it by eating and drinking more. Of course, this is just my guess. I don't really know what happened that day, except that I survived when I shouldn't have.

I can only speculate on it, but what I can truly tell you is that it changed me. I got a second chance in life that day. At that point, I don't know what mattered except that I woke up for a reason. I don't know what it looked like from the outside, but it just felt like I fell asleep and woke without having any control of it. I believe that I didn't do anything to deserve mercy that day but God extended it to me. I am not perfect and in fact I have fallen short of it many times. I am truly sorry to those that have encountered me when I was not the best version of myself. I may sometimes have come out a little rough, but I am a sinner and guilty of it. That day made me realize how feeble and nothing I was. I hope that I never forget that day and let pride slip in again.

I am forever thankful. May we all be humble, thankful and recognize that we're deserving of nothing. Let us exist for one another. Thank you for reading this book. May God's blessing and peace be with you always.

CONCLUSION

F lying through the warm air with true tenacity the arrow only disappoints when it misses the mark. The villagers trudge on after it. Word had spread from hut to hut and around the morning fires that there was a leopard in the area and killing their sheep. The best hunters found the rumors to be true. My uncles Elisha and Amin were leading a team to track the animal.

They tracked and tracked until sure enough they found it. They assembled the team. Some of the men would take the attack approach, while others stood back in defense in case the leopard went around them. My two uncles took the role of archers. If one was going to release an arrow to the animal, they had to hit it in the perfect spot. If they miss slightly and only injure the leopard, it would get angry and come after them. If the wind blew ever so slightly in the direction of the leopard it would be able to smell them and attack, so they must approach quietly and with great stealth.

My uncle climbed up the nearest tree. He hid in between the straggling branches. He spotted the animal climbing up the ridge line. With strong arms he pulled out the bow from his sack that he had strung around his waist and put it to good use. With just one arrow released, he nailed the leopard in its side. The men could see it tumbling down to the ground below, and he knew it was finished.

Just as the hunters were about to celebrate, the leopard just as quick as it fell, got up again. Even as he could taste his own death, he fought. It began to thrash and tear at everything it could see. It was as if it realized that death had come upon him and instead of surrender, he chose to thrash. He clawed at everything he could see and howled with every ounce of energy that remained. The villagers have a way to describe a man who acts like a leopard in this way. May we not claw on the bark of a tree as our life here on earth ends. May our days be so filled, our hours so content, that when our time does come, we have nothing left vacant than that which is to come.

ABOUT THE AUTHOR

S am Chelanga is married to his wife, Marybeth, and together they have three boys: Micah, Joseph, and Jeremiah. Sam was born and raised with his eleven brothers and sisters in a remote village in rural

Baringo County, Kenya. Growing up, a typical day for Sam would be spent waking up early to milk the cows and make fire for the morning tea, walking to school, and trekking through the hills to fetch water and till the land.

Against all odds, after high school he ran his way to becoming a collegiate track and field record holder and national champion in the United States. After eight years as a Nike Professional Track and Field Athlete, he surprised the world when he retired to become a soldier in the US Army. Sam and his family currently live in Columbia, SC while he works as a Platoon Leader at Fort Jackson.